A Baby's Viewpoint of Life and Death

"…and by it he [she] being dead yet speaketh." Hebrews 11:4

ANITA LOVATO
JAMES WILKINS

A Baby's Viewpoint of Life and Death

"…and by it he [she] being dead yet speaketh." Hebrews 11:4

ANITA LOVATO
JAMES WILKINS

ISBN # 978-1-61119-055-7

Printed by Calvary Publishing
A Ministry of Parker Memorial Baptist Church
1902 East Cavanaugh Road, Lansing, Michigan 48910
www.CalvaryPublishing.org

Calvary PUBLISHING
FOR BAPTISTS
BY BAPTISTS
CP
KJV
A ministry of Parker Memorial Baptist Church
1902 East Cavanaugh Road • Lansing, Michigan 48910
Phone: 517.882.2112 • Fax: 517.882.2317
www.calvarypublishing.org

Gracie Lovato
Mora, New Mexico
July20, 2005 – May 13, 2011

This sweet little girl loved to sing,
The B-I-B-L-E
That's the book for me
I stand alone on the Word of God
The B-I-B-L-E
BIBLE!!!

Another one of her favorite songs was:

Jesus loves me, this I know
For the BIBLE tells me so.
Little ones to him belong,
We are weak but he is strong.
Yes, Jesus loves me
Yes, Jesus loves me
Yes, Jesus loves me
The Bible tells me so!

Although Gracie didn't know how to explain the Scriptures, the Bible teaches that every person is sent into the world for a distinct purpose.

The Bible which she sang about gives the lessons that God wanted us to learn from Gracie's life. As her friend and older brother in the Lord, God allowed me to be the instrument to reveal them.

Our prayer is
May her little life touch the lives of many and bring the peace, comfort and salvation which Gracie experienced.

A gift of Comfort
Presented to

_____

By Someone Who Cares

_____

_____

A short personal message

_____

Date

"To every thing there is a season, and a time to every purpose under the heaven: A time to be born, and a time to die; ... "
Ecclesiastes 3:1-2a

CHAPTER ONE
EACH LIFE HAS A PURPOSE

A BRIEF VISIT TO EARTH

Recently, I attended the funeral of a friend of mine. I marveled at how beautiful she was, laying there in her casket surrounded by all of her favorite stuffed animals, just sleeping. Gracie's short race through life didn't even reach her sixth birthday....**then she was gone!**

My mind questioned, "What was Gracie's purpose? What message was God attempting to communicate to the world through her brief appearance on earth?"

> II Timothy 1:9 "Who hath saved us, and called [us] with an holy calling, not according to our works, but **according to his own purpose and grace,** which was given us in Christ Jesus before the world began," (1)

Since God had to override my own dear mothers attempt in her deep state of bereavement and confusion to abort me I am very aware that God has a distinct purpose for everyone's life. Apostle Paul made this point very clear in his letter to young Timothy.(1)

When God struck Paul down in conviction on the road to Damascus he proclaimed, "I have appeared unto thee for this purpose."(2)

In a day when the nation of Israel had rebelled against God and turned a deaf ear to God's prophets he used a man's life to illustrate his message. Much of the book of Hosea reveals God's illustrated message to his people. (3)

In today's society where the Lord's Day [Sunday] has become just another day in the week and the Bible is looked down on it would be very possible for God to send another illustrated message through the short life of a little girl?

Hosea 1:2 "The beginning of the word of the LORD by Hosea. And the LORD said to Hosea, Go, take unto thee a wife of whoredoms and children of whoredoms: for the land hath committed great whoredom, [departing] from the LORD."
(3)

THE SHORT MINISTRY OF JOHN THE BAPTIST

Jesus said of all the people around him there was none greater then John the Baptist.

"There was a man sent from God, whose name was John."
John 1:6
(4)

There are several scriptures which announce the purpose of John's life. He was sent to prepare the way before Jesus first coming. He was to baptize Jesus and introduce him to the nation of Israel. (4)

As God began to move in my mind and I pondered these questions, I thought, "Why not let **Gracie answer these questions and tell her story**, regardless of how brief it may have been?"

Before we get to her message we will introduce her and the family which God chose for her to be a part of.

"Now faith is the substance of things hoped for, the evidence of things not seen."
Hebrews 11:1

Chapter Two
A Mothers Version of
Gracie's Troubled Life

The Bible states that one's life on this earth is as "a story that is told". The following chapter is a brief summary of Gracie's life as told by her mother perfectly illustrated that truth.

God prepared a special little person and sent her into the world. Her life impacted every person she encountered. Now she is gone... but her influence lingers on.

Listen to her story as told by her mother, Anita Lovato.

CONCERN FOR MY BABY
May 2005

My friend and mid-wife, Sheri Raphaelson, came to our home for a pre-natal checkup because I was concerned that the baby was only moving twice a day. This did not seem normal as I was 28 weeks along in my pregnancy and my uterus should have measured 28 weeks, however the uterus measured 35 weeks instead. At the end of the appointment, Sheri is certain the size discrepancy of my uterus is a definite sign that my baby could be born with complications; complications which include: Spina Bifida, swallow and brain problems. For a moment, in my heart I worried, and then God gave me immediate peace. I remembered telling Sheri that whatever God's will was for my baby, we would trust Him. After my check-up, Sheri scheduled an ultrasound appointment to check for any noticeable abnormalities, and I am faced with the possibility of not being able to give birth at home. When the ultrasound was completed at Santa Fe Imaging, nothing was found abnormal with the baby. The baby was the right size, the bag had the right amount of water, and everything measured and looked normal. Throughout the pregnancy I was sure I was having a boy and I wanted to confirm this through the ultrasound test, but Jake did not want to know the sex of the baby. He enjoyed the surprise of waiting till the birth, because we both knew whether our baby was a boy or girl, he or she would truly be a blessing. However, I continued to believe I was having a boy. As we left Santa Fe, we thanked God for the normal test results of the ultrasound and continued to prepare for home delivery of our soon to come baby.

Months after this ultrasound and Gracie's birth, Sheri who is also a lawyer, sent a letter to Santa Fe Imaging explaining the condition and complications of Gracie's birth, and their response to the letter was that no test is ever 100% accurate. That day, God had hidden the true results of Gracie's condition—even from the medical experts who could have revealed her abnormalities. Through it all God was working his perfect plan for her life.

LABOR BEGINS EARLY THIS MORNING
July 20, 2005

Early on the morning of July 20th, I started the labor process in order to give birth to my new baby, and I am still certain the new addition to our family will be a boy. We had previously decided he (the new baby) would be named, Isaac Judah, which means laughter-praise in the Hebrew translation. For each of the pregnancies of the previous six children I would ask the Lord to give me a scripture to meditate on for the duration of each labor, and that morning I asked the Lord for something I could use to comfort myself as I would undergo the labor and birth of my baby, either a song, Bible verse, or a prayer. When I opened my Bible, God led me to II Corinthians 12:9, as I pondered on this verse, I questioned the Lord asking Him, "I already know this verse, Lord," (I had memorized this verse in 2001 quoting it to my mother-in-law, Carlota Lovato, before she underwent heart surgery) and the Lord said to me, "This is the one I want you to think about today." II Corinthians 12:9 reads, "My grace is sufficient for thee: for my strength is made perfect in weakness. Most gladly therefore will I rather glory in my infirmities, that the power of Christ may rest upon me." Upon reading this scripture, I felt the Lord piercing my heart about the infirmities, yet I thought of the heavy labor I would soon endure, and assumed that was the infirmity God was showing me--I never related the infirmities to my baby. (Just recently I looked up the meaning of infirmity and it was the description of Gracie's life, how Powerful God is!)

MY BABY IS BORN
July 20th, 9:20 pm.

After several hours of labor, my baby is born! Sheri immediately wrapped the baby in receiving blankets and the baby was warmly placed in the arms of Esther, my daughter, who at the time was fifteen years old. Previously, after each birth of my children, Sheri would quickly wrap each baby and sometimes in the excitement of the birth we did not see if a boy or girl had been born. This night, I did not check the sex of my new baby, yet I assumed this was my boy. However, to my surprise, Esther excitedly proclaims, "It's a girl!" For the first time in twelve pregnancies, I had not chosen a girl's name. The kids began to ask, "What is her name Mom?" As I mentioned earlier, I was positive this was a boy, so a girl's name was not on our list. I told the children that I would need to pray about her name and that I would have one by the next day. When I finally held my beautiful baby girl, all bundled in her blankets, I truly felt blessed to hold my 12th bundle of joy, not yet realizing just how mightily she would be used by God—not only in my and my family's lives, but in the lives of others as well.

As I looked at her little fingers poking out of the blanket, they were all I could see, I realized how different they seemed. Also, her cry, at birth, was not the same tone of my other newborns and I thought within myself, "This baby seems different, but it is probably all in my mind." When I attempted nursing her, she was unable to create suction, so I looked in her mouth. She seemed to have what looked like soft pink teeth. I asked Sheri to come over and look at her, and when she examined the baby's mouth, Sheri explained that it appeared my baby had a cleft palate. Immediately, Jake and Emilee, my second-oldest daughter, went to Walmart to buy baby bottles and formula in order to nourish the baby. Meanwhile Sheri began a full examination of the baby and discovered numerous health issues. After Jake and

Emilee returned with the feeding supplies for the baby, a bottle was prepared for her, but when she is given the bottle to suck, she is still unable to create suction. By now, Sheri is sure the baby will need to be admitted to the Los Alamos Medical Center, with specific care from Dr. Jaqueline Krohn, the pediatrician we chose for all of our children. I tried overhearing Sheri in the next room, but she spoke very quietly so I could not hear the abnormalities concerning the baby and the diagnosis. When I knew the baby was headed for the hospital, I wanted to go in with her, however, because of complications I suffered after the birth I was told to stay home and drink fluids to accomodate the severe blood loss I experienced. Jake did not give me a choice of going and I had no choice but to stay behind to rest and pray—which was very difficult for me to do.

We made preparations for the baby to be taken to the hospital in Los Alamos, NM, and around 1:30 am Jake and Esther were ready for the trip. The children asked again for the baby's name, but I did not have one just yet. Since we needed to admit her to the hospital, I needed to decide on a name. After several suggestions, I began to think of II Corinthians 12:9, and the parts of the verse that read, "My Grace is sufficient... and most gladly therefore will I rather Glory in my infirmities," and that was it. I decided that her name would be Grace Glory Lovato. So my baby was admitted to the Los Alamos Medical Center on July 21, as Grace Lovato. For myself, it was a very long night to pass the time worrying about the well-being of my infant, but morning finally came. The day of the 21st, I anxiously awaited word from Jake about Grace, and when he finally called to give a report and diagnosis from Dr. Krohn, I was shocked to hear that Grace had been born with extensive infirmities—infirmities I never anticipated she would possess. Jake and I discussed the extent of Gracie's abnormalities which continued with a swollen fontanel (soft spot), club foot (on both feet), cleft palate, deaf in both ears and the probability of being mentally delayed

> Grace was now diagnosed with a heart defect, swollen Fontanel, hand and foot contractures, Cleft Palate, Club Foot, deaf in both ears and probably mentally retarded with some form of Syndrome.

with some form of a syndrome. And her little hands that I thought were different also had defects. I could not believe what I was hearing, yet as I discussed Grace's condition with Jake, I began to realize why God had pierced my heart the morning of my labor when I read II Cor. 12:9. God, in His omniscient (all-knowing) way had impressed, on my heart, what I truly believe was Gracie's condition at birth. I immediately asked Jake to come home and take me to the hospital. Although we did not know, Dr. Krohn already knew Grace would face heart issues because of a loud heart murmur she could hear and an enlarged liver she could feel.

As I waited for Jake to come home and take me to the hospital, I thought of the name Grace Glory and the scripture in II Corinthians. Jake had a great-great grandmother named Altagracia Lovato and a grandmother named Altagracia Trujillo, and as I thought more, I felt that Grace's legal name should be changed to Altagracia, and her middle name, Glory, changed to Gloria, which in Spanish means Heaven. Altagracia Gloria Lovato: Grace on High Heaven Lovato. If I had planned for Gracie's name it would never have been Altagracia or Grace. There was a pretty little girl by the name of Grace Sandoval at our church, so I never thought to name our baby Grace and the name Altagracia was not to my liking. After deciding on Altagracia Gloria, I knew this name was of the Lord and not of my own choosing—and later, the name was perfect and proved appropriate for her, according to her life. God had given her this name. After Jake arrived home, and we were headed back to the hospital, I revealed my desire to change Grace's legal name to Altagracia Gloria, and he was pleased with the change. That night I stayed with Grace at the hospital, and the next morning Dr. Krohn began making arrangements for Grace to be transferred to UNM Hospital in Albuquerque, NM. Dr. Krohn explained the reason for Grace's transfer to UNM, was because of the heart murmur she could hear, and began to talk of heart surgery in California at Stanford University. I, Jake, and Esther were concerned and began to prepare ourselves for what was ahead in Albuquerque and California.

On July 22nd, I waited all day for word from Dr. Krohn about a transfer to UNM Hospital, but it never came. Apparently the cardiologist at UNM, who Dr. Krohn spoke with, recommended we make an appointment for Monday, July 25th, with Dr. Krohn, in order to perform an EKG (in order to confirm the heart defect) and hearing test on Grace. We were puzzled with the response from the UNM doctor, because of the urgency of a heart defect, but did not question UNM's decision against an immediate transfer. We were discharged from the hospital on Friday, July 22, 2005, so we took our sweet little baby home, not realizing the trial that was ahead.

LIFE IS SO DIFFICULT

July 25th—Dr. Jacqueline Krohn's Office

On Monday, the 25th, we returned to Dr. Krohn's office for Gracie's EKG and hearing tests. When the EKG turned up with irregularities, again Dr. Krohn addressed the possibility of taking Gracie to Stanford University in California for heart surgery—Dr. Krohn was positive Gracie was facing heart issues. By now, Gracie's liver was very enlarged, which was the absolute sign that Gracie had a heart defect. After several newborn-hearing tests, which Gracie failed (each one), it was confirmed she was deaf. It was hard not to cry, but I told Dr. Krohn that since Grace was deaf we would learn sign language and do our best to take care of her every need. I questioned Dr. Krohn about Grace's mental condition, and her response was; because of Grace's high pitched cry, it was very likely she was mentally delayed. Even though the future looked grim, I had peace that everything was going to be okay. I knew that no matter what the outcome, I would love this baby despite her condition. Later, Dr. Krohn faxed the EKG test results to the cardiologist at UNM Hospital, who then made an appointment the following day for Gracie to be seen in his office. Again, we were concerned of the delay to send Grace to UNM Hospital, so I asked Dr. Krohn to call the doctor and request that Grace be seen this same day. We expressed that we trusted Dr. Krohn's concern and shared the urgency she had for Grace to be seen by a cardiologist, and that we were prepared to go the very same day to UNM if need be. However, the cardiologist told Dr. Krohn that the appointment for the next day would be fine—I later found out about a miscommunication between the two doctors of Grace's true diagnosis, and that was the reason for the delay of her appointment to UNM.

July 26th—UNM Children's Heart Center: Albuquerque, NM

On Tuesday, July 26th, after the appointment with Dr. Waldman, the cardiologist at UNM Hospital, Grace is confirmed to have a Double Outlet Right Ventricle heart defect with a Ventricular Septal Defect (VSD)—a hole between the ventricular heart chambers. This VSD saved Grace's life allowing her to remain alive inside my womb. With this heart condition, Grace had two right ventricles instead of a normal left and right ventricle. A normal heart operates using the right ventricle to circulate blood into and through the lungs (to be oxygenized) which then flows though the left ventricle, exits, and enters the body. Since Grace had two right ventricles, there was no way for the blood, after being circulated through the lungs, to enter the body. Without a left ventricle, Grace would not have oxygenated blood flow into her body, and therefore would have never survived in my womb. However, the VSD defect allowed the blood to overflow and drain into the body. What we first saw as a defect to Grace's heart, God had actually used this defect to spare her life while forming in my womb—this was yet another miracle of God in this little baby's life. While in Dr. Waldman's office, a genetics doctor had been called to perform some blood tests on Grace, but she never arrived. However, right as we were preparing to leave Dr. Waldman's office, the genetics doctor walked into his office. As the doctor attempted to draw blood from Grace, for the test, and was unable to draw enough blood, she realized that Grace was highly dehydrated. Thank God this doctor arrived when she did, because we were not aware because of the cleft palate, Grace had not been receiving the nourishment we thought she was getting all along. So that evening Grace was admitted into the

Pediatric Intensive Care Unit (PICU) at UNM Hospital.

SO MUCH TRAUMA TO MY SWEET BABY
July 26th – August 9th UNM PICU

While at UNM, Grace underwent multiple tests in attempts to diagnose all of her infirmities, besides the heart defect. During this time, my sweet little baby went through so much trauma, but through it all she remained strong— a little fighter. I remember singing the words to a hymn, that to this very day I still wonder where I learned the words. It was the chorus and tune to "Marvelous Grace." I would sing;

> *I would sing;*
> *"Grace, Grace,*
> *God's Grace,*
> *Grace that will*
> *pardon and*
> *sanctify me.*
> *Grace, Grace,*
> *God's Grace,*
> *Grace that is*
> *greater than all*
> *my sin."*

> *"Grace, Grace, God's Grace, grace that will pardon and*

sanctify me. Grace, Grace, God's Grace, Grace that is greater than all my sin."

Later I found that the words I sang were not the same as the original hymn, yet had the same meaning. I would sing this song to Grace in order to calm myself, because I figured she could not hear me sing since she had been proclaimed deaf while at Los Alamos Medical Center. However, one day while I was holding Grace, staring into her eyes and weeping, Esther, who had come to the hospital to stay with me, asked, "Why are you crying, Mom," and I answered, "Because my baby is deaf". Esther responded by saying, "How can she be deaf, if she calms down every time you sing that song (Marvelous Grace chorus) to her?" The thought had never occurred to me, but Esther was right. Every time I would sing to Grace, usually when she was whimpering after being poked by a needle, she would immediately calm down and begin to fall asleep. I had been so blinded by the negative results of Grace's hearing tests, that I did not realize she had been hearing my voice the whole

> *I locked Grace and myself in my room, and wept, praying to God about all my fears and doubts.*

time. (Is this not how we sometimes react and respond to God during our trials in life?)

In my desperation for answers after Grace's birth, because of the six failed hearing tests, I would ask if there was a possibility that Grace had fluid in her ears. But it was explained that the tests administered for her hearing, were tested using brain waves and quite accurate, and this was the reason for concluding Grace was deaf. Yet, later testing of Grace's hearing proved Grace only had a slight hearing loss. I truly believe, with all of my heart, that God had healed her little ears and she <u>was</u> able to hear (another miracle).

During this two week period at UNM, it was concluded that although Grace had the Double Outlet Right Ventricle with a VSD heart defect and other infirmities, the genetic testing showed that Grace had no syndrome— which the doctors assumed Grace had a syndrome because of all the infirmities she had.   Also, each infirmity proved to be less extensive than what we originally thought when Grace was born, and we praised God for the good news.   The results of Grace's infirmities were: no club foot, just certain foot deformities; hand contractures, that only time would tell the affects (Grace later proved she could do almost anything with her hands as if normal); the cleft palate was not as severe as we originally thought, but was a soft sub-mucous palate (which could be easily fixed, but not necessary); and mentally, there was still a question about a mental delay.

WHY DIDN'T SHE DIE AT BIRTH?
One week before Heart Surgery

After spending around two weeks at UNM, we were released from UNM Hospital one week before going to Lucile Packard Children's Hospital in California for heart surgery. After a few weeks of the hustle and bustle of hospital life, when I finally got home the devastation, fatigue, and discouragement I felt—for myself and Grace—was overwhelming and I found it very hard to practice my faith in God. Sometimes in our walk with the Lord, we get so caught up in what we can see, that we fail to remember our faith is based on what we cannot see (Hebrews 11:1). In my case, I had front row seating in the life of Grace; for weeks I watched and thanked God for the miracles He was performing in and through Grace, yet I still doubted. After returning home, I locked myself and Grace in my bedroom for what seemed like hours of weeping and praying to God about all of my fears and doubts. One day I finally asked God, "Why did you send Grace like this?" This notion

> I asked, "Why not let her die in my womb?" "Why let her be born?" or "Why didn't she die at birth?"

ran through my mind constantly and of course God already knew my heart and my thoughts before I asked him this question. I knew I could not hide my feelings from Him, so I asked, "Why not let her die in my womb, Lord?", "Why let her be born?", or "Why didn't she die at birth?" I told the Lord that I was not embarrassed of my baby, but I knew the suffering she would endure in this life. This hurt me and was a trying time for me because I knew life was going to be difficult for her. Although I questioned God's reasoning for what Grace, and our family were going through, I remembered later, when all was well with Grace, to ask God's forgiveness for not trusting Him, for not having the faith to believe that He was in control. I thanked the Lord for listening, but not acting upon, my foolish doubts and questions.

CODE BLUE
August 21st – Heart Surgery in California

Finally, on August 16th, we flew from New Mexico to California for Grace's heart surgery. The heart surgery was performed by Dr. Mohan Reddy at Lucile Packard Children's Hospital in California and went well. However, while Grace was in recovery, something goes wrong. On Sunday, August 21st, Grace Code Blues in the early morning hours and is resuscitated back to life after Dr. Gayle Wright and her staff feverishly work on her for almost 3 hours. Around 5:45 am, Jake received a telephone call informing him of Grace's survival despite suffering a code blue. By God's mercy, Grace survives again and we are released from the hospital to go home three weeks later.

September 2005

At home in Alcalde, NM, while feeding, Grace began choking and stops breathing. We immediately call 911, and an ambulance is dispatched to our house. Before the ambulance arrived at our house, I cried out to the children that Grace was dead. Grace had stopped breathing and become stiff in my arms, and since I was still on the phone with the 911 operator I followed her instructions of what to do for the emergency. Right before the ambulance arrived, I was able to revive Grace. Again, the Lord protects Grace.

> *Right before the ambulance arrived, I was able to revive Grace.*

October 2005

While at UNM Hospital, in July, Grace developed feeding issues after being flooded by an unmonitored feeding pump, which resulted in Pulmonary Edema (fluid in the lungs). Because Grace's formula was made too strong, she would constantly vomit. This added to her diagnosis: Feeding issues requiring a twenty-four feeding pump and the G-tube. We now had a baby who was unable to tolerate normal bottle feedings, and Grace received a G-tube for feeding and ear tubes to drain the fluid.

January 2006

Grace's physical therapist Jean Porteus PT, notices a scoliosis curve in her back.

February 2006
Grace's heart is starting to show signs of obstruction and her Blood pressure is rising out of the normal.

June 2006
Dr. Bosch, orthopedic doctor, confirms Grace has scoliosis.

August 2006
After an ECHO (heart ultrasound) it is noted that the obstruction is worse.

September 2006
A heart catheterization is ordered, showing both ventricular openings are obstructed with scar tissue from Grace's previous heart surgery. Dr. Waldman schedules Grace to return to Lucile Packard Children's Hospital in California for a second heart surgery.

October 2006

The second heart surgery is performed by Dr. Mohan Reddy, to remove scar tissue that is obstructing both ventricular openings and to remove scar tissue from the VSD. The conductive center line to the ventricles is damaged causing a 4th degree heart block, the worst form of heart block a heart patient can experience. Grace is given an external pacemaker to keep her ventricle heart rhythm beating. Five days later the doctor determines that Grace has lost this

The conductive center line to the ventricle is cut causing a 4th degree heart block. The worst form of heart block

heart beat forever. She receives a Pacemaker and becomes 100% Pacemaker dependent. God gives the song **"Wonderful Peace,"** my favorite verse to sing to Grace was:

I am resting tonight in this wonderful peace
Resting sweetly in Jesus control
For I'm kept from all danger by night and by day
And His glory is flooding my soul!
Peace, Peace wonderful peace
Coming down from the Father above
Sweep over my spirit forever I pray
In fathomless billows of love!

While Grace was in recovery, we were not allowed to stay in Grace's room at night and the separation was horrible but I knew when I left Grace every night that she was in the Lord's hands. One night I asked God for a scripture to read to Grace before I left her and He led me to Psalm 57. As I came to verse 7, I read, "My heart is fixed, O God, my heart is fixed, I will sing and give praise." I was so excited when I read this verse because I thought God was going to fix Grace's heart, or so I thought. I had been pleading with the Lord for days that he would heal Grace's heart. I really felt that this was the answer, but soon realized that God was telling me that this was the way Grace's heart was fixed— with a pacemaker. It was set to stay blocked without a heartbeat. In verse 7 of Psalm 57, the Lord says to "sing and give praise," although I found it difficult to trust God, I knew I must praise Him for allowing her to survive yet another surgery, and she was healed. So I sang a praise song to Him before I left the hospital.

We continued with numerous doctors visits in the years to come, and I learned through this long and difficult road, that constant discernment from the Lord was necessary to know what to do for my precious little girl. Through it all, Hebrews 11:1 came alive to me, this scripture reads, "Now faith is the substance of things hoped for, the evidence of things not seen." Grace had truly become a faith child, because **we never knew how her body or organs were doing, we could only trust that God knew and was in control.** From then on, I found myself in constant prayer asking God to heal this child my way, **if it were His will.** I did not realize when I asked God for healing or to do His will in Grace's life, that I was asking Him to make the choice of healing her my way or taking her home and

> *Grace had become a true faith child. We never knew how her body or organs were doing, we could only trust that God knew and was in control.*

healing her in His way (God's ways are **always** right and perfect).

THE SHRINERS HAD COMPASSION ON GRACE

In March of 2009, a couple from our church, Al and Fran Garcia, felt Gracie needed help, so they told their daughter, Jeanie Powell about their concerns for Gracie, and asked if we had ever been to a Shriner's Hospital. We had always heard of many Hospitals for Gracie, but hearing and contacting them was a different story. Fran and Al explained how Jeanie could help us apply to Shriner's for help, however, as time went on, I had forgotten all about the application process. In early June of 2009, Jeanie called to tell us that some good friends of hers from Albuquerque Shriner's Balud Abyad sponsors were coming with a large group to meet at the Sierra Bonita Camp & RV Park (about 17 miles from where we presently live in Mora, NM)—which Jeanie and her husband Kelly own. Jeanie asked if we could meet with these sponsors on Saturday morning June 20, 2009, and we were glad they could meet with us that day. We arrived at 11:00 am, a little nervous because a lot of the families there were on vacation, I felt as if we would be interrupting their day. Jeanie introduced us to Orvis Creel and Jim Shepherd, who made us feel welcomed. When they heard about Grace, their overwhelming concern for her health issues was such a blessing. As we talked, they watched sweet little Gracie sitting by my side, and you could see the compassion in their eyes they felt for her. They gave me an application to fill out in order to request an evaluation of Gracie's orthopedic needs, because it was obvious how severe her scoliosis had become.

It seemed as though we were there for at least two hours, and yet they never treated us as if we were in their way or ruining their day. When we left, Orvis came over with a huge box of muffins for all of us, and thanked us for coming. That ended up being such a blessing to Grace and all of us, and a few weeks later we received a call from Dr. Norman Otsuka, with the Los Angeles, CA-Shriner's Hospital. He was requesting records for Gracie. He went on to tell me that Gracie's application for care had been hand delivered to his office early Wednesday morning, on June 24th, which was four days after meeting Orvis Creel and Jim Sherpherd at Sierra Bonita Camp. Creel and Shepherd had made a trip to the Los Angeles Hospital and were there at Dr. Otsuka's office first thing in the morning waiting for the doctor to arrive. They told the doctor of Gracie and her desperate need of immediate help. When I heard of their urgency to submit the application immediately, I could not help but break out into tears knowing the love and concern these two men felt for Gracie. Later on, to our disappointment the Los Angeles, Chicago, and St. Louis Shriner's Hospitals rejected Gracie because of her heart condition. However, one day when Creel was attending a special meeting in Arizona, he saw Dr. Otsuka. Dr. Otsuka asked how his little patient (Grace) was doing, and Orvis explained, "Not too well." He told of all the Shriner's

Hospitals that had been contacted concerning Gracie, but could not help her because of her heart condition. The Director for the Sacramento Shriner's Hospital overheard the conversation and said he would look at her records and consider seeing her in their hospital. It was done! Yet again, **God intervened on Gracie's behalf**.

Our next trip took us to Sacramento in October of 2009 to meet with Dr. Joel Lerman, a doctor of Orthopedics at Shriner's Hospital in Sacramento. We could see his passion for helping children in need because of the kindness he showed to Grace and us. Dr. Lermen did a full evaluation of Gracie and knew by examining her that there was a Neurological problem. He wrote his report and noted four diagnoses on Gracie's severe scoliosis, which were: Tethered Spinal Cord, Syrinx, Chiari

Malformation or Lipomeningocele (These were the same conditions which concerned Sheri Raphaelson during my pregnancy, God had given Sheri discernment). Dr. Lermen sent us back to New Mexico for a Myelogram of the spine to check for the spinal cord/brain issues. Back at Carrie Tingley Hospital, under the direction of Dr. Elizabeth Szalay, a regular CT scan was ordered and done in December 2009. However, this test was not the correct test we needed. A Myelogram consists of putting dye in Gracie's spine while conducting the CT scan—this test was finally done in February 2010, and confirmed that Grace had a Tethered Spinal Cord. This was the cause of her now very severe scoliosis. Through constant prayer, God sent us to a

> *I often had to be that advocate through prayer for Grace, asking the Lord constantly for His discernment in treatment.*

faraway place and used people he placed in our path to reveal this critical health condition in Gracie's spinal cord. Who but God could have planned it all so perfectly? In July 2010, we made one more trip to Shriner's of Sacramento to a follow-up appointment to check the results of the spinal cord being released. Dr. Lerman explained Gracie's lot in life was not fair, and that we had two surgical options for her. Both procedures would not be good for Grace and both would be high risk and change her life for all of her future. Dr. Lermen also mentioned having other patients as Gracie with a spine like hers and are healthy, and others with straight spines that are very unhealthy. That day we chose to trust God with her spine and that He would bring the healing, or the cure.

HER SPINAL COLUMN WAS ROTATED 50 PERCENT
August 2010,

In August 2010, we traveled to Colorado Children's Hospital in Aurora, CO hoping for a second opinion, in hopes of better news. We met with Dr. Mark Erickson, MD-Chairman of Orthopedic Surgery, who did an extensive 3D CT Scan of Grace's spine. He found that Grace had a very severe curve and her spinal column was rotated fifty percent on the bottom. He also did not have a good diagnosis or treatment plan for Grace. Again, we had two surgical options that would not be healthy for Gracie, both procedures would stop Gracie's upper torso from growing normal and one procedure had a 20 percent probability of paralysis. Dr. Erickson gave the two surgical options or the option of doing nothing at all. So, again we chose to do nothing at all, trusting that the Lord had the healing.

Once again God brought us to a place where he held the key to the healing or curing of her back and rightfully so. Sometimes we put our trust in man, when ultimately everything is in God's control. I prayed constantly for healing from the Lord or for His will to be done. I often worried about seeing all the different doctors and the possibilities of ending up with the wrong doctor or hospital that might make a mistake which could cause unnecessary harm or

> We see now that this was the right decision, not knowing her life would abruptly end in May 2011.

suffering for Grace. I often had to be the advocate for Grace, through prayer, asking the Lord constantly for His discernment and wisdom in her treatment. I felt God had shown us his power and mercy by allowing both Dr. Lerman and Dr.Erickson, who did not know about each other, had never met or discussed Grace's condition to conclude that we could choose to do nothing about her spine. This allowed us to leave everything in God's hands, and we see now that this was the right decision, because we did not know then that her life would abruptly end on May 13, 2011. God spared Grace from the suffering involved with either surgical option for her scoliosis. Through it all, we always see the goodness of God.

ANOTHER DEFECT THAT GOD HAD PLACED FOR GRACIE'S GOOD
March 2010

Grace undergoes surgery at UNM Hospital with Dr. Erich Marchand, Pediatric Neurologist. Dr. Marchand performed the surgery to release the tethered Spinal Cord that was diagnosed earlier by Dr. Joel Lerman of Shriner's Hospital. This entailed Dr. Marchand surgically cutting through Grace's L3 section of her lower back, drilling through the bone, and carefully removing fatty tissue that confined her spinal cord in the L3 position of her lower back. After the procedure, Dr. Marchand came to the waiting room to inform that the surgery was successful and Grace was in recovery. He explained how the spinal cord had retracted beautifully when released, and when he was cutting through the skin on her back to begin drilling through the bone in order to reach the spinal cord, he found a defect in the bony area of a soft tissue and not bone. Dr. Marchand was pleased to find that the soft tissue eliminated the drilling of bone to reach the spinal cord, thus making the surgical procedure uncomplicated. This was just another defect in our eyes that God had placed for Gracie's good. Out of all of the specialists Gracie had seen, none of them noted this defect beforehand but Dr. Jacqeline Krohn, Gracie's PCP.

February 2011

In February of this year, we took Gracie to her annual heart check-up and Grace is given an excellent report concerning her heart. Her cardiologist, Dr. J. Deane Waldman of UNM Children's Heart Center, told me and Jake that aside from Gracie being pacemaker dependent, her heart was in excellent condition, and we praised God for this result. Again, God had proven the concept of faith in Hebrews 11:1. We never knew the condition of Gracie's heart by physically looking at Gracie, yet we always hoped and prayed that it would stand the test of time (God always proves faithful through whatever we go through).

GRACE KNEW SHE WAS GOING TO DIE
May 13, 2011

On Friday, May 13th, Grace is sure it is her birthday, and throughout the day informs Seth, her nine year old brother, that today is her birthday. Grace played as usual with the kids, but seemed a little more tired that day, she laid around watching movies till the evening. In the latter part of the evening, Grace began to struggle breathing, her eyelids began to swell and her heart rate was fluctuating in a very abnormal way. Grace was taken, by ambulance, to Alta Vista Regional Medical Center in Las Vegas, NM which is about forty-two miles from our home in Holman, NM. When she arrived to the hospital, Grace was in cardiac arrest and it was at the hospital Grace went home to be with the Lord a few minutes before midnight. This happened exactly one month ago, at this same hour that I am writing this story. The pain at times seems unbearable, but GOD IS *ALWAYS* GOOD!

MAMA, REMEMBER WHEN I DIED?

A few months before Gracie's death she found a Gospel tract entitled,

Somebody Loves Me, it is printed by Chick Publications in cartoon format. In this tract a little boy dies, and is taken up to heaven by an angel. She was very saddened by the death of this little boy and Grace would cry as we read this to her and she viewed the pictures, but she carried it around everywhere for those couple of weeks—even sleeping with it under her cheek. Later, we received another tract entitled, *Tiny Shoes.* One night before bed, when I first read this book to Grace, she called herself, Juanito, the little boy in the Story, and I was Juanito's mother. As I read the story to her, we came to the part where Juanito dies. Grace opened her teary eyes and looked at me and silently cried, but said nothing. She lay down and placed the tract under her cheek and fell asleep. The next morning she asked Jacob, Josiah and Abigail her older brothers and sister to read it to her again, and each one acted out the parts of the characters in the story. In the story, once Juanito has died, his shoes are hanging on his grave maker at his burial, and later that morning Gracie tied the laces of her sneakers in a knot and hung them on the headboard of our bed. I remember the week before Gracie died, she said to me."Mama, remember when I died?" I asked her, "Gracie when do you remember when you died?" but she never answered me. Again I asked, "When did you die Gracie?" but she ignored me and walked off.

Throughout Gracie's life, her story of struggle, hope, faith, and miracles has been told hundreds of times. She was prayed for by so many people and everywhere we would go people would ask for Grace and how she was doing. We always gave God the Glory for the miracles He was working in and through her because it was God who kept this little girl in the palm of His hand. Many of Gracie's therapists always noted that she was amazing and a miracle; one physical therapist, Jean Porteus from Espanola, NM told me that Gracie had beaten the odds; Connie McGhee, another physical therapist from Santa Fe, told of her 30 years as a physical therapist and how she has worked with several children with healthier backs than Gracie yet they were unable to walk, but Gracie rode a bike, walked and played as normal as possible for her. Grace especially loved ponies, and would ride the ponies at the State Fair, circus, or even the carousel in the shopping mall as often as she could. Grace touched so many lives as she lived and has continued to touch lives in her death.

> *God used her with her infirmities to glorify himself and show His power and strength through her.*

Now I understand the part of II Cor. 12:9b, that reads, "Most gladly therefore will I rather glory in my infirmities, that the power of Christ may rest upon me." God used Grace's infirmities to glorify himself and show His power and strength through her.

BY GOD'S GRACE, GRACIE
GENTLY FELL ASLEEP

I thank the Lord that through her sudden and untimely death on May 13, 2011, God answered a prayer I questioned Him about in August of 2005. With little faith in my trial after Gracie's

> *"As I prayed for her all I could see was her running, dancing, and skipping all over Heaven, talking, singing, and laughing as she longed to do in this life."*

birth, I worried that my child would suffer in this life. By God's grace she gently fell asleep the night she died. I

Thank the Lord that he took her without suffering; I thank Him for not allowing her to suffer in the almost six years of her life on this earth, and for never bringing me to the point of pleading with Him to take her because of the suffering. God is Gracious, Merciful and Longsuffering because He LOVES each and every one of us. Thank God He allowed her to live such a full and joyful life, Praise be to God!

Anita would sing Laura Story – "Blessings" to bring herself comfort after Gracie's passing.

We pray for blessings
We pray for peace
Comfort for family, protection while we sleep
We pray for healing, for prosperity
We pray for Your mighty hand to ease our suffering
All the while, you hear each spoken need
Yet love us way too much to give us lesser things

Cause what if Your blessings come through
raindrops
What if Your healing comes through tears
What if a thousand sleepless nights
Are what it takes to know You're near
What if trials of this life are Your mercies in
disguise

We pray for wisdom
Your voice to hear
And we cry in anger when we cannot feel You near
We doubt Your goodness, we doubt Your love
As if every promise from Your Word is not enough
All the while, You hear each desperate plea
And long that we'd have faith to believe

Cause what if Your blessings come through
raindrops
What if Your healing comes through tears
What if a thousand sleepless nights
Are what it takes to know You're near

What if trials of this life are Your mercies in disguise

When friends betray us
When darkness seems to win
We know the pain reminds this heart
That this is not, this is not our home
It's not our Home

Cause what if Your blessings come through raindrops
What if Your healing comes through tears
What if a thousand sleepless nights
Are what it takes to know You're near

What if my greatest disappointments
Or the aching of this life
Is the revealing of a greater thirst this world can't satisfy

And what if trials of this life
The Rain, the storms, the hardest nights
Are Your mercies in disguise

Used by permission.

"Yea; have ye never read, Out of the
mouth of babes and sucklings thou
hast perfected praise?"
Matthew 21:16

Chapter Three
THE PREACHERS' VERSION

THE HOME SHE WAS TO VISIT

In the light of eternity little Gracie's visit to this earth would be so short it would
take a trained eye to catch the bleep on the radar screen as she briefly appeared on the earth.

She came into the home of Jake and Anita Lovato on July 20th, 2005 and left just as suddenly on May 13, 2011. Time, which has been described as "measured eternity" and has been

illustrated as a small dot on an endless line which has no
end or beginning. In the light of this there would be no way to register that she ever existed..

Even in contrast to a human life of 70 or 80 years, her little race of 5 years, 10 months and 23days, would go unnoticed by all but a very few people. **That is, if she wasn't a chosen vessel with a message from God.**

She was born at home in Alcalde, New Mexico which is so small that only a few local people in Northern New Mexico have ever heard of it. A small little person of 6 pounds and 12 ounces in a crippled body was welcomed into a large family of eleven brothers and sisters. Perhaps no one ever received as much love as Gracie received from the members who made up the loving family of Jake and Anita Lovato and their twelve children. Gracie was under watchful, loving care almost 24/7 for each and every day of her entire life.

THE MID-WIFE'S CONCERN

The mid-wife who was known and respected for her unusual sense of discernment and medical ability was troubled as she examined little Gracie while she was still in her mother's womb. Upon voicing this concern Anita went into the clinic and had extensive tests. Anita was assured by the reports and the hospital staff that Gracie was normal and that there was nothing to worry about.

> Perhaps no one ever received as much love as Gracie received from the members who made up the loving family of Jake and Anita Lovato and their eleven children. Gracie was under watchful, loving care almost 24/7 for each and every day of her entire life.

This did not reassure the mid-wife, and Jake got the impression that the mid-wife had grave doubts and was very concerned that the baby had severe problems.

After Gracie was born, the mid-wife sent a report to the hospital that stated the following problems which Gracie had.

GOD GAVE THE NAME "GRACE"

Recent tests and the latest's indicators to Anita Lovato had convinced her that her soon to be born baby would have severe complications. Since all of her other children had normal births and were healthy babies this was uncharted waters for her. But Anita

> When she and Jake became born again Christians they agreed to cut up their credit cards and live by faith.

didn't focus on circumstances and potential dangers because her faith was in the Living God. When she and Jake became born again Christians **they agreed to cut up their credit cards and live by faith.** At first it was very hard. Many of their family members and friends strongly voiced their opinions against such a far out, fanatical way of life. But God really blessed their faith over the twenty year period since they made that commitment so it was only natural for Anita to turn to God and His Word for direction.

When she began to pray God confirmed that in truth, the baby would have grave complications. With this knowledge God also brought to Anita's mind a scripture which God enabled Apostle Paul to endure and overcome his extreme health problems. The words which God spoke to Paul are, "**My grace**

is sufficient for thee for my strength is made perfect in weakness." II Cor 12:9

The impression upon Anita's heart did two things, it calmed her completely and give her courage that whatever would happen God would work it out for good.

The second thing was just as real as God's comforting peace. God impressed upon Anita's heart that if the baby was deformed or mentally challenged that **she would accept it as God's will and would be proud of the child** and give it what loving care that was needed.

Little did Anita know that she and her family would have to rely so heavily on God's grace during the next almost six years with the many trips to the hospitals and little Gracie's' **two deaths**.

There would be many anxious moments, tears and long nights for Anita and her family, but they found that God promise which he so personally impressed on Anita's heart that night was true. **His Grace was sufficient and it was demonstrated every day** as little Gracie came into their lives and lived among them.

Anita and her husband Jake, although they had sonograms done before the baby was born didn't ever inquire whether the baby would be a boy or girl. They believed that baby was a gift from God. Anita believed that she would have another boy so she had picked out a name for a boy.

When a little girl arrived Anita did not have girls name picked out. So when the baby arrived with deformed feet and a hole in the roof of her mouth which made it impossible for her to feed, the

Scripture which had given her so much assurance before came back into her mind. It was so comforting and vivid that Anita knew it was from the Lord. She would name the baby, **Grace.** The Spanish name for Grace is Alta Gracia which literally means **Grace on High or grace on high heaven,** Anita accepted her tiny little gift from God and **by relying upon God's amazing grace,** she would help her precious baby to fulfill that purpose.

GRACIES' FIRST DEATH

Gracie arrived on this earth with two defects in her heart. There were two arteries going into the right chamber of her heart and none going into the left chamber of her

The surgery was successful but two days later Gracie stopped breathing. **A code blue** was ordered and the staff worked feverishly for almost three hours before Gracie started breathing again.

heart. Normally this would mean that the baby would die in its mother's womb, but little Gracie also had a defect in the bottom of the right side which allowed some blood to enter the left side of her heart.

Friday August 19, 2005 at the Lucille Salter Packard children's hospital in Palo Alto, California Gracie had heart surgery to correct these defects. The surgery was successful but two days later Gracie stopped breathing. A code blue was ordered and the **staff worked feverishly for almost three hours before Gracie started breathing again.**

A LITTLE GIRL WHO SHOULD NOT HAVE LIVED

This was the opinion of one of the many doctors which ministered to Gracie. In addition to her heart defects, her deformed feet, and the hole in the roof of her mouth, she had extreme high blood pressure. They also thought she was mentally retarded. Surgery, when she was three weeks old where they put tubes in her ears and stomach corrected her high blood pressure. One of the major defects which was not detected **until she was four years old** and had severely plagued her was that her spinal cord was attached to the boney area of the lower back which caused her spine to have severe curvatures both at the top and the bottom. Again, Surgery greatly released the tension on the Spinal Column.

PACE MAKER FOR GRACIE

In October, 2006 Anita and Jake were back at Lucille Salter Packard children's hospital where little Gracie received a pace

According to the specialist she should have been "a little more than a vegetable or at least confined to a wheel chair."

maker. Gracie was a patient in **Los**

Alamos, Las Vegas, Palo Alto, California, The New Mexico University Hospital, Albuquerque NM, Sacramento, California and Denver Colorado and had six major surgeries. According to the specialist she should have been "a little more than a vegetable or at least confined to a wheel chair." But after the detachment of her spinal cord Gracie became a "walking miracle." She would roll around on the floor and play with her brothers and sisters. They would assist her as she learned not only to walk but to dance also. Everyone was amazed and delighted as she even learned to ride her bicycle. The physical therapist who worked with her could not believe it.

When they tested her IQ **it was higher than children her own age**.

> The Holy Spirit comes in and lives in a child until the child comes to the age of accountability

But where this crippled little girl excelled was in the spiritual realm. She loved it when someone would read to her about Jesus.

THE SPIRITUAL DEVELOPMENT OF GRACIE

Gracie's love to have someone read to her about Jesus was only natural because **the Holy Spirit comes in and lives in a child until the child comes to the age of accountability** when they learn the difference between right and wrong. When they consciously sin, the Holy Spirit withdraws. This also means that the baby would go to Heaven when it died **without the aid of baptism, prayers or any other ritual**. The death of Jesus on the cross was accepted by God as payment for their sins.

> For thou hast possessed my reins: thou hast covered me in my mother's womb.
> Psalm 139:13

The other reason she loved to hear about Jesus is because **she had heard**

about Jesus while she was still in the womb of her mother. **She had heard about Jesus** while she lay in a hospital in a strange city. **She had heard about Jesus** for hours on end as her mother would quote

> Anita believed that the Bible was a living word which brought healing and life to people,

Scriptures or sing quietly to Gracie as she lay recovering from her latest surgery. Hearing about Jesus or songs about Jesus was a way of life. Anita believed that the Bible was a living word which brought healing and life to people, therefore the endless Scriptures and songs.

Anita quoted the twenty-four verses in Psalm 139 to Gracie almost every day. There were some days when Gracie lay between life and death and no one knew if she would live or die. Then Anita quoted it over and over again.

There is no person Gracie's age that ever heard so much about God and His power and goodness as Gracie did. Some days Gracie was ministered to by her mother eight to ten hours a day. **In crucial times, more.**

> Thine eyes did see my substance, **yet being unperfect; and in thy book all my members were written,** which in continuance were fashioned, when as yet there was none of them.
> Psalm 139:16

Gracie could quote some of the verses which she had heard so many times. Anita was teaching Gracie to memorize the whole chapter of Romans twelve when she died.

TO WALK BY FAITH

God had taught Jake and Anita to walk and trust Him by faith, preparing them to trust Him and endure the many trials while they loved and taught little Gracie.

SOMEONE LOVES ME AND TINY SHOES

In January 2011 five months before she died the family received some Chick Tracks through the mail. A Chick Tract is a gospel tract which features both pictures as well as the message of Salvation. In reality it is a small booklet about 20 pages long. The two chick booklets which Gracie had her brothers and sisters read to her over and over again were "Someone Loves Me" and "Tiny Shoes."

"Someone Loves Me" was about a poor dying boy. Before he died he learned that Jesus loved him. He prayed the sinner's prayer and among the last pictures were the angels carrying him up to heaven.

The booklet entitled "Tiny Shoes" was about a poor little boy who had no shoes. His father promised to buy him some shoes but each week his dad would either drink or gamble his money away. Finally the little boy became sick and went out into the wintery storm looking for his dad and his new shoes.

The last picture showed the tiny shoes tied together hanging over a cross which was made into a tombstone.

The little boy died in the storm while praying to Jesus. The father finally bought the shoes only to find his little boy dead. The last picture showed the tiny shoes tied together hanging over a cross which was made into a tombstone.

Little Gracie would go to bed each night clutching the two booklet tracts.

Sometimes when she had someone read the tracts to her tears would well up in her eyes, other times she would silently weep.

Later she would have her brothers and sisters act out the parts in these two booklets. She would play the part of the two little boys who died. She would say, **"that's me mama that me"** referring to which ever booklet they were reading or dramatizing. But then she would point to Juanito's father and exclaim, **"That's not my daddy! That's not my daddy! My daddy is good!"**

She would say, **"that's me mama that me"** referring to which ever booklet they were reading or dramatizing.

"MAMA, DO YOU REMEMBER WHEN I DIED?"

These are the words which Gracie startled Anita with on April 28th, two weeks before she died.

Anita asked, "What did you say?"

Again Gracie repeated, "Mama, do you remember when I died?"

Anita answered, yes, I remember. Why do you ask?

Gracie retreated into her bashful state and walked off to join her brothers and sisters.

The same week Anita came into her bedroom to find that Gracie had tied her shoe strings together and hung them on the bed post of her mother's bed.

The day that Gracie died her brothers and sisters came into her room and **found her in a kneeling position on** her knees much like the little boy in Tiny Shoes when he died.

"IT'S MY BIRTHDAY TODAY!"

Little Gracie had a premonition that she was going to die. She told her brother, "Today is my birthday!" She knew well that her literal birthday would not be until July 20th. The family made Gracie's birthday about the biggest day of the year. They had already talked about her birthday which would not be for another two months.

> "Today is a special, special day for me." Since her birthday was always a special, special day, Grace used the word birthday instead of the word death.

Gracie was saying, "Today is a special, special day for me." Since her birthday was always a special, special day, Grace used the word birthday instead of the word death. Just as the

Apostle Paul, referring to his death, stated, "My departure [for Heaven] is at hand." I have fought a good fight, I have finished my course...in essence...my purpose on earth is over and I am going to be with Jesus.

Little Gracie, thinking about her special, special day exclaimed, "Today is my birthday!" A few hours later, she gently went home to be with Jesus.

THE HUMAN ELEMENT IN GRACIE'S LIFE

Little Gracie's eleven brothers and sisters accepted her into their lives as a special gift from God. There is no one that knows the Lovato family who ever heard one of her large family even complain or act in a contrary way toward Gracie. She was the most loved and cared for little girl that, perhaps ever lived.

In the weeks and weeks of confinement in different hospitals often times the little infant hovered between life and death, her mother was right by her side. Anita would quote scripture to Gracie or softly sing

This same nurse told Anita that the love, singing and quoting the scriptures had caused her to rededicate her life and get back into church.

little songs of hope and faith to her. Several hospitals staff members were deeply moved by Anita's devotion and practice. One particular nurse came in each day and announced, **"Miss Gracie, Miss Beverly is here to watch over you today."** This same nurse told Anita that the love, singing and quoting the scriptures had caused her to rededicate her life and get back into church. Little Gracie was proving to be the blessing which her heavenly father had sent her to be as her little twisted body lay in a strange city far , far from home.

Alta Gracia, a name given by God which means grace on high heaven, was giving her heavenly father pleasure while moving adults closer to God and heaven through the grace which he supplied to Anita whose only thought was toward her responsible to comfort and encourage her baby.

A WORD OF COMFORT
I am so sorry to hear about Gracie's passing. She was such a special little girl. Even with all of her physical problems, she was so strong and determined...I can picture Gracie now, as a young girl with a straight spine, dancing and playing in Heaven.
Dr. Jacqueline A Krohn, MD, MPH

"By faith Abel offered unto God a more excellent sacrifice … and by it he being dead yet speaketh."
Hebrews 11:4

Chapter Four
Gracie's Victorious Life

Please listen very closely as this tiny little person speaks....

Mother, when God sent me into the world, you made great preparations for my arrival. You fixed a special place for me, bought me new clothes, and gave me a special name. And Mother, I love my name, Gracie.

The moment I was born they placed me upon your breast and it was so reassuring to me. After the traumatic experience of being born --- all the commotion and bright lights --- then I heard your voice;

It was so reassuring!

As I was caught up close to you – I heard your heart beating…. It was the same beat I had heard when I was part of you.

I began to feel secure – then the tones of love in your voice –
I was glad to be alive.

Oh sweet mother, you did your best to welcome me into this world --- and it was wonderful!

"…the beggar died, and was carried by the angels into Abraham's bosom:…" (Luke 16:22).

Your best was motivated by human love.

But oh mother dear --- my reception into heaven ---- It was breath taking.

I was carried up to heaven by the gentle hands of the angels. (1)

I left my weak imperfect body for a "body not made with hands, eternal in the heavens."(2) And oh mother, the special place God prepared for me is beyond the ability of the tongue to describe. There is no other place in all of heaven like it, and **it's for me... your little child**. I can't wait to show it to you.

> "For we know that if our earthly house of this tabernacle were dissolved,... **an house not made with hands, eternal in the heavens."**
> II Cor 5:1
> (2)

And oh mother, you tried your best to make our home a place of love, warmth, and beauty and it was to me a little heaven on earth, BUT MOTHER, THIS IS THE REAL HEAVEN – the love here is beyond description...(3) so warm, real, and wonderful --- and the beauty of heaven is beyond imagination. Mother, if you took all the beautiful sunsets, mountains, and glorious landscapes, it would be nothing in comparison to the beauty of my new home and country where I now live.

> "Eye has not seen, nor ear heard, neither entered into the hearts of **men what God has prepared for them that love him.**"
> *(I Cor. 2:9)*
> *(3)*

Mother, you wanted me secure and mother, there is nothing to hurt or harm me in my new homeland.

You longed for me to have a great education... I learned more the first moment I arrived here than any mortal tongue is able to teach in a lifetime.

Mother, you longed for me to have the very best! What more could a kid want than to walk on the streets of gold surrounded by family members and friends as we travel on our endless adventure through heaven?

REMINDERS FROM GOD

But mother the purpose of my little life was to remind you of some of the lessons you already know.

First, the reason God sent me into the world was to remind you that I was a gift of God to you and to the world. (4) Mother you may be wondering why I only lived a very short time on earth. God sent me into the world to remind you of some things

> "Every good gift... cometh down from the Father..." (James 1:7)
>
> "...which lighteth every man that cometh into the world." (John 1:9) (4)

you already know. He sent me to demonstrate His unconditional love for us.

Remember Mother, how the love God placed in me, **drew people to surround me** and it made them feel good afterwards? That was a demonstration of God's love. God was loving people

> "...one day is with the Lord as a thousand years…" *II Peter 3:8*
>
> "For a thousand years in thy sight are but as yesterday when it is past, and as a watch in the night."
> *Psalm 90:4*
> (5)

through me, your little girl. Mother that love permeates all of heaven. God's love is sweeter than any rose or flower on God's great earth. I breath in that great love with every breath I take. Mother it is wonderful!

Second, my short life was to remind people of how brief our earthly phase on this earth really is as we journey into eternity.(5) Death does not end all, it is only a door for, (a child of God), to enter into God's glorious eternity.

God attempts to communicate in the Bible that 1,000 years on earth in his sight is as one day. 1000 years in his sight is as yesterday when it is past, or even as a three hour watch in the night. My little short life was to illustrate that one's life is like a vapor or puff of smoke or a short story, **like the ones you used to read to me.**

A lifetime mother can best be illustrated by what **we did every night**. You kissed me goodnight, turned off the lights, and suddenly you were kissing me good morning. That is how brief your life is mother.

My appearance on the earth was to try and impress on people that whether they live an hour, ten years, or even seventy or eighty years, their life is like a story that is told and will very soon be over. After God reminded the palmist of this truth, David cried out, "Teach us to number our days that we may apply our hearts to wisdom."

A lifetime mother can best be illustrated by what **we did every night**. You kissed me

> "Man that is born of a woman is of few days, and full of trouble." *Job 14:1* (6)

goodnight, turned off the lights, and suddenly you were kissing me good morning. That is how brief your life is mother.

Third, I was sent into the **world to demonstrate that life is a struggle.** (6) My short struggle illustrates that man lives in a world governed by the devil who brings death and destruction into the lives of all mankind. It is the devil which wrecks hopes and dreams and brings despair into people's lives. It is he who brings arguments, harsh words and divisions between family members. In such a world, God promises to work all things together for good to the people

> "...**all things work together for good** to them that love God..." *Romans 8:28*
>
> "...worketh for us a far more exceeding and eternal weight of glory;" *II Cor 4:17*
> *(7)*

who love Him and are called according to His purpose. It is God who comforts and gives purpose. (7)

God also promised that the light affliction which we suffer, such as my sickness and death, **would work out for our eternal good** and blessing.

Mother, my loving Heavenly Father sent me INTO YOUR LIFE FOR YOUR ETERNAL GOOD. I know it hurts very badly right now since I am gone and you can't see any good from my short visit, but let my tender and loving Savior help you. He is the God of all comfort and grace and he promises to stick closer to you than any brother and will never leave you or forsake you. He is the God of all grace and wants to comfort and help you, please mother, just call out to Him! He is there and he will help you.

My many trips to the hospitals, the surgeries and my struggle just to live illustrates the hard times the devil gives to all people. But, mother to live in God's great house where he rules is best described by one word, "Heaven!"

Fourth, we were all sent into

"...for thou hast created all things, and for thy pleasure they are and were created."
Revelation 4:11

..." do all to the glory of God."
I Cor 10:31
(8)

the world for a purpose. Often times we human beings lose our focus. When we do, God has to send a little reminder, (like me), into the world to help us find our real purpose. Our real work in life is not to please ourselves, but to please and give God pleasure.

God's word states that we are to give God glory in everything we do. (8) Jesus told his disciples that they were in the world, but they were not of the world. Our purpose on the earth is not to live for our pleasure, we **are not to work to lay up riches** by accumulating material things on this earth, but we are to lay up treasures in heaven by giving the Gospel to people and getting them saved. (9)

The night I died my beautiful oldest sister Annie almost died. An elk

> "Lay not up for yourselves treasures upon earth,..."
> Matthew 6:19-20
> (9)

ran in front of her car and caused a wreck which totaled her car. Mother, I died because I had fulfilled my purpose. Annie was spared because **God still had work for her to do**.

Fifth, mother, I was sent into the world to remind people in a vivid way that **there is life after one dies, physically.** Mother, you don't think of me as being annihilated and decaying in a cold dark grave, but you think of me as being alive!

I am alive, mother, I am alive! God made me in His image and likeness and since He is an eternal being, He made me an eternal

"And the LORD God formed man of the dust of the ground, and breathed into his nostrils the breath of life; and man became a living soul. "
Genesis 2:9

"...Let us make man in our image, after our likeness: "
Genesis 1:26
(10)

being that will live forever. (10)

That's the reason I had you read over and over again the stores of death in the Chick Tracks. We all die mother. We all need to prepare for death which will happen to all of us. That's the reason, mother I would cry out as we read the stories of the two tracks. **"That's me, mother, that's me."**

We must learn to live our lives in the light of our soon coming death.
When Adam sinned it brought death which means separation from God. God gave His Son to die on the cross to pay for a person's sins and to redeem sinful man back to Himself. His sacrificial death paid for the **sins of the innocent, like**

> "Who gave **himself a ransom** for all..."
> *Timothy 2:6*
>
> "...who is the **Saviour of all men**, specially of those that believe." *I Timothy 4:10*
> *(11)*

me, and for the sins of all those who do not have the mental ability to choose. (11) All others, because we are all sinners, must hear of God's love and provision for them in order to be saved from eternal separation from God in hell. Each person must have their sins paid for personally, either by dying and going to hell or by accepting God's loving payment of His son, Jesus, who died as their substitute.

Mother, there is life after physical death for each person on the earth. Some will join me and experience the exuberant life with God in heaven, while others will sink down, down into the blackness of darkness, lost and without hope in a devil's hell

"For the wages [*payment*] of sin is death..."
Romans 3:23

"For he hath made him to be sin for us..." *II Cor 5:21*
(12)

forever. (12**) My mission from God was to remind you of this reality.** Mother, the only sad thing about my funeral was that I was saying good bye to so many who **are trusting in their religion or in themselves**, instead of Jesus in order to get to heaven. It made me sad to think that I will never see them again. Oh, I wish they could have the peace and eternal life I am enjoying.

The reason I was clutching the two Chick Tracks, so closely in my hands and slept with them as my pillow **was to illustrate my faith in Jesus Christ as my Saviour**. I was trying to tell people how precious Jesus was and to rest in him alone as their Saviour.

I'M ON VACATION IN HEAVEN

Mother, it is wrong when a person dies for people to say, "He has gone on to his reward." That is not what the Bible teaches. It says, blessed or happy is the person who dies in the Lord. They rest from their labor (they have gone on vacation), but their works do follow them.

The works he is talking about are the results or works which the person who died, life produced. Mother, like miss Beverly, the nurse who rededicated her life and became active in serving Jesus again. Whatever works she does for the Lord – like getting people saved. Part of the reward she receives will go to our account in heaven.

If my brother and sisters, even my uncle and aunts (whom God used my life to touch) began to serve and work for the Lord – Mother, part of the reward will go to our account and enrich our position in the 1000 year reign with Jesus when he comes back.

Mother, that is almost to marvelous to believe but it is true because God's Word said it is true.

Sixth, mother, one of the main reasons God took me from you so early was because he loved me so much and wanted to spare me of an "**evil to come**."

Mother, God knows everything! He sees the end from the beginning. God saw something terrible coming up a little later in my life, which I would not have been able to bear. It would have totally destroyed me. Mother, it would have greatly damaged or destroyed your life also. So my loving Father reached down and lifted his little child up above "**the evil to come**."

Mother, when you saw me resting in my little casket

> "...the righteous is taken away from the evil to come."
> *Isaiah 57:1-2*
> *(13)*

with all our wonderful, loving memories unsoiled by some "**evil to come**," it was because our loving Father wanted to spare you of the sorrows that the **evil to come** would have caused you. Your sweet little baby was lifted up safely **above the evil to come** and is eagerly waiting to welcome you to my new mansion. (13) **Mother, isn't God wonderful?**

Oh yes mother, I met another person who has no name when I arrived. He asked me to share the lesson from his life with you also. He said that his story brought joy and hope into the lives of thousands.

Mother, I have met so many fascinating people since I got here; preachers, prophets and this special young man who has a story to tell.

He died when he was **only a new born baby**. He even took me and introduced me to his father. He was one of the greeters who were assigned as part of my welcoming committee when I arrived in heaven. He doesn't have a human name, mother, but he loves to introduce himself as the only one of King David's sons who does not have a name. He then joyfully expresses just call me, "Messenger Boy".

His mother and father committed the awful sin of adultery which resulted in his birth. He only lived a few days before the angels carried him to paradise. Mother, even though his mother and father sinned **there was no reflection of shame cast upon him.**

His father,

> "But now he is dead, wherefore should I fast? can I bring him back again? I shall go to him, but he shall not return to me. "
> *II Samuel 12:23 (14)*

King David, loved him just as you loved me, mother. From the time "Little Messenger Boy" was born until he died his father fasted and begged God to let him live. When Little Messenger Boy left for paradise David got up, bathed, ate and went in and worshiped God. When the king's servants inquired of David about his total about-face of his actions from one of tears and anguish to peace and composure, little messenger boy's father made the following explanation.

"While my son was alive I begged God to forgive me and let me keep him. But when God said "no" and took him to Paradise I knew he was alive and that I would soon join him in heaven, (Paradise). My answer to my servants and to the world was, "I cannot bring him back but I can go to where he is, (Paradise). He is safely home and waiting for me in heaven. (14)

Mother, my new friend, "Little Messenger Boy's" message is to all mothers and fathers; we kids and babies are well and happy in heaven and regardless of what you did, **especially to the mother who aborted their babies**, we love you and yearn to welcome you to come to our home in heaven.

THANK YOU MOTHER

Mother, I just want to thank you for singing to me. In my little mind I would be scared and wonder, "What's going on?" Then you would begin to sing, "Grace, Grace, God's grace...and within another verse or two I would realize everything is ok. Mama and God are watching over me and mother, when you would quote the whole 139th Psalm. In my little mind I would silently be saying them with you.

It was so good and reassuring when I finally realized that God saw me developing in your womb and **gave me the exact body he wanted me to have**. And mother, he gave me the exact mother who would love me and help me to fulfill my purpose on earth. Isn't God good

"But we see Jesus, who was made a little lower than the angels for the suffering of death, crowned with glory and honour; that he by the grace of God should taste death for every man. "Hebrews 2:9(15)

mother? But how could you know fully...you still have a limited knowledge – But oh mother – you will soon join me here – and then you will know.

DON'T BE AFRAID

Because Jesus tasted death for everyone of his children, mother, there is nothing to be afraid of when a child of God dies.(15) The truth is mother, a child of God never dies. When his

"We are confident, I say, and willing rather to be absent from the body, and to be present with the Lord. "
II Corinthians 5:8(16)

earthly race is over, he takes his last breath on earth followed by his next breath in heaven.(16)

One of my new friends described his death by saying, "I was just walking along and took one step on earth, the next step in mid-air and my third step was "on the streets of Gold!"

> **Paul's Testimony**
> "For I am now ready to be offered, and the time of my departure [death] is at hand."
> II Timothy 4:6(17)

Apostle Paul described his death as a departure from the earth.(17) While the apostle Peter described his death as one who was changing clothes.

Mother, the first Christian martyr, Stephen, while being stoned to death saw Jesus standing in an open door

> And they stoned Stephen, calling upon God, and saying, Lord Jesus, receive my spirit...And when he had said this, he fell asleep.
> Acts 7:59-60 (18)

in heaven, and said, "Lord Jesus, receive my spirit" and then went to heaven (18)

Lastly, mother, I want to leave a little poem with you that one of my new friends in heaven wrote. I have changed it a little and addressed it directly to you.

> Peter's Testimony
> "Knowing that shortly I must put off this my tabernacle,[by dying] even as our Lord Jesus Christ hath shewed me"
> II Peter 1:14 (19)

Please read it mother – it will be a blessing to you.

MOTHER, I AM SAFELY HOME
I am home in Heaven, Mother,
Oh, so happy and so bright,
There is perfect joy and beauty
In this everlasting light.

All my pain and grief is over,
Every restless tossing passed.
I am now at peace forever,
Safely home in Heaven at last.

Mother, you must not grieve so sorely
For I love you dearly still,
Try to look beyond earth's shadows,
And learn to trust our Father's will.

Mother, try to learn the lessons I tell
**And remember Jesus died, to save
sinners from hell.
Look at Our loved ones still lost
And, tell them the story of the cross.**

There is work still waiting for you,
So now you must not idly stand.
Do it now while life remaineth,
Soon you shall rest in Jesus' land.

Mother, when your work is all completed
He will gently call you, "come."
Oh! The rapture of that meeting
Oh! The joy to see you HOME.

(Author Unknown)
(Adapted by James Wilkins)

Remember Mother, **I am more alive in
heaven than I ever was while on the earth.**

And mother, if people learn and do from the lessons I taught it will bring us greater rewards in the Millennium.

Everyone's life is as a tale
that is told –People
should ask themselves,
Is my story all about me?
Or is it all about Jesus?

FOR THE DOUBTERS

I can hear someone say, "Gracie, a little six year old kid didn't have the ability to teach all those things which the preacher wrote about.

Let me ask you a few questions?

Does God send each person into the world for a distinct purpose?

The Bible says "**yes**!"

Could her little troubled life be used as an illustration that every life is brief and is a story which is told; full of trouble?

The Bible says "**Yes**!"

Does the bible teach that everything and everyone was created to being God pleasure and to give him glory?

The Bible says "**Yes**!"

Does the Bible state that God works all things together for good to them who love him and are called according to his purpose?

The Bible says "**Yes**!"

Does the Bible teach that God paid the price for the sin of the innocence?

The Bible states, "**Yes**!"

If God loves you and wants you to reconcile to Him and spend eternity with Him in Heaven, wouldn't He use every means to communicate, even a little crippled girl?

The Bible states, "**Yes**."

Please, **please, PLEASE**, let His love through this little girl reach your heart!

EPILOGUE

FOR THOSE WHO LOST A BABY

The most devastating even in the life of a couple is the loss of a child especially if the child is an infant.

The divorce rate especially among young couples are very high. This is because each spouse grieves differently from each other and since they both are grieving they can not give proper comfort to each other.

The wife gives over to weeping and emotional outbursts, while the husband grieves inwardly. This leads to the wife believing that her husband is hardened and doesn't share her grief. Nothing could be further from the truth. He is unable to express himself in a way the wife perceives his bereavement.

The husband attempts to comfort his wife in her uncontrolled weeping, but after four or five outburst he becomes confused and no longer seems to be sympathetic.

Please seek help and comfort from the Lord. Little Gracie's lessons are the very ones your little one would give you if she was able to communicate with you.

Your child (under age of accountability) is in heaven. The child is alive and is praying for you. The child loves you even though you may not have been as good a parent as you could have been. God hears the child's prayers and shares the child love and concern for you.

The only difference is God is able to hear your prayers and give you healing and comfort.

For those who may need help in wording their prayers please pray these words as sincerely as you can.

Dear Heavenly Father,

Please forgive me of all my sins, Jesus, come into my life and heal me of my broken heart. Forgive me and save me so I can be reunited with my child when I die.

I will go to a church who preachers the Bible so I can learn of you and receive comfort and complete healing. Thank you so much. Amen.

WORD FROM THE AUTHORS
If you need further understanding we have three other books which have brought healing and comfort to many.

Healing Words for Hurting People.
Healing Words for Lonely People
Wilt Thou Be Made Whole? – An eight week self help course to spiritual and mental healing.

Visit our Website for more information.
www.JamesWilkins.org